UPRISING & RESISTANCE

FOR THE AFRICANS WHO FOUGHT FOR FREEDOM ON THE SHIPS OF THE MIDDLE PASSAGE

Edited by
Gboyega Odubanjo

Published by Ink Sweat & Tears Press
in association with Spread the Word
and Black Beyond Data

London 2023

Editor: Gboyega Odubanjo
Typeset by Starfish, Norwich
Printed and bound by Page Bros, Norwich

Saidiya Hartman. 'Intimate History, Radical Narrative'
The Journal of African American History 106, no. 1 (Winter 2021): 127-135, https://doi.org/10.1086/712019

Saidiya Hartman, 'On Working with Archives: An Interview with Writer Saidiya Hartman'
First published 18 April 2018 by *The Creative Independent*.
https://thecreativeindependent.com/people/saidiya-hartman-on-working-with-archives

Derek Walcott, The Nobel Prize Lecture © The Nobel Foundation 1992

ISBN 978-0-9927253-7-2

In memory of all enslaved Africans of the Middle Passage, including those who revolted against their enslavement on board ships, and of those on shore who risked their own safety to come to their aid.

As much as violence, brutality and dehumanising conditions were ever-present aboard slave ships, so was resistance to that inhumanity. Kidnapped and enslaved people fought against their capture and enslavement constantly. It is estimated that as many as one in ten or even one in five slaving ships experienced a significant insurrection during the voyage from the coasts of Africa to the Americas. While we know that they occurred we have little documentary evidence of what transpired. Despite unimaginable odds people resisted the conditions of their commodification at every turn. We need poetry and art to give life and meaning to these moments where historical evidence cannot.

— Alexandre White

The *Uprising & Resistance* project is managed by Spread the Word and the project publisher is Ink Sweat & Tears Press. All funding was provided by Black Beyond Data, Johns Hopkins University and the generous support of the Mellon Foundation.

Lloyd's provided access to its archives which gave the poets and artists the historical records needed to further understand the role the insurance industry played in the trade in enslaved people. *Uprising & Resistance* allows Lloyd's the opportunity to confront the global impact and violence of its legacy.

TABLE OF CONTENTS

1.	Introduction	9
2.	Keith Jarrett	11
3.	Remi Graves	21
4.	Levi Naidu-Mitchell	29
5.	Jess Nash	37
6.	Courtney Conrad	45
7.	malakaï sargeant	53
8.	Notes & Glossary	63
9.	Bios	65
10.	Core Partners	66

INTRODUCTION

When we think about the markets of the trans-Atlantic slave trade and that 400-year-long trafficking of African lives, we oftentimes turn our gaze to the slave castles, forts and factories off the coast of West Africa, where captured people were forced from their homeland. From here, we might begin thinking about the various markets across the Americas, where people were bought for labour, reproductive capacity and sold for various commodities. But too often we neglect the insurance and financial markets of London, Liverpool and Bristol at our peril. These are locations geographically distant to the Americas, where the public imagination locates the trade in enslaved people, but which we now understand to be responsible for creating spaces of exchange and economic speculation that were necessary to turn the wheel of the industry.

This volume is the result of a set of collaborations that are part of a wider project to shed light on the critical roles that City of London merchants, financiers and underwriters played in the British trans-Atlantic slave trade. In 2022, we began examining the Lloyd's of London Collection, archives and objects from the market long presumed by historians like Joseph Inikori and Eric Williams to be the central space for the insurance of slaving voyages bound from Britain. This was part of a financially independent research collaboration between Lloyd's and Black Beyond Data, a Mellon Foundation funded project based at Johns Hopkins University. Like the chains, shackles and instruments of direct violence that are so evocatively recalled demonstrating the atrocities of slavery, these economic and financial systems exploited human beings, rationalised tearing apart families, seizing children and usurping bodies and wombs for profit. These systems were as central to the carrying out of the trans-Atlantic slave trade as those technologies of direct violence.

This project will appear in two parts. The historical research will be presented in a series of digital exhibits under *Underwriting Souls*. In addition, working with Tom MacAndrew and Ruth Harrison from Spread the Word, Kate Birch of Ink Sweat & Tears, and editor Gboyega Odubanjo, we have shared the research with young Black poets and artists for the second part of the project: *Uprising & Resistance*. In the resonance of the Lutine Bell, which sounded out loss across the Lloyd's insurance market, there is the resounding silence of the names, voices and experiences of the enslaved. The task of poets and artists is to transgenerationally resurrect them, so we can at last see, hear and feel them.

A pivotal source from the Lloyd's Collection are the insurance agreements for the 1794 voyage of the Guipúzcoa. In August of 1794, Fermin de Tastet, a Spanish merchant in the City of London, walked to the Royal Exchange which housed the Lloyd's insurance market at the time to seek insurance coverage for a slaving voyage. He sought insurance coverage for the voyage from:

Liverpool to the Coast of Africa, during her stay & trade there,

and from hence to her port or ports of discharge on the Island of

Cuba.

de Tastet, working on behalf of Havana based merchant and slave ship owner Sebastian de Lasa y Irala, procured two agreements from the Underwriters at Lloyd's, one totalling '£3500.00 for the ship' and 'each slave valued at £45 each'. Over twenty underwriters would sign the agreements; among them were future Lord Mayors of London, Members of Parliament, and some of the wealthiest merchants in Britain. Some of these people were known to be the most prominent traders of the era. Some also owned plantations in the Americas. Some were the operators of slaving factories – the ports of no return where Africans would be imprisoned before they were exchanged for goods and loaded aboard ships borne for the Americas.

The experiences and the voices of those bound within the Guipúzcoa were erased. We don't know what sort of lives these people made for themselves. These materials tell us much, but for as much as they tell us about those who orchestrated the traffic and enslavement of African people, their business relations and their activities, they cannot recover the lives and histories of those kidnapped and trafficked for chattel slavery. We are merely left with fragments, beneath which the pentimento of thousands of documents imprint their absence.

The poet and philosopher Derek Walcott wrote in his Nobel Prize acceptance speech on the promise of cultural production in the Caribbean, amid its roots in the genocide of indigenous peoples, forced and coerced colonial migration, and the kidnapping, trafficking and enslaving of Africans: 'Break a vase, and the love that reassembles the fragments is stronger than that love which took its symmetry for granted when it was whole.' From historical scholarship, we know that enslaved people resisted their dehumanisation and commodification at every turn. Though we may not be able to return their voices to the world, we can lean on our imagination in ways that challenge how we see the world, the blinders we affix, and the possibilities for our future. Where history loses form, art and poetry take shape. That is the vision of this volume.

Victoria Lane, Pyar Seth and Alexandre White

KEITH JARRETT

The True Briton, Dawson, from Bonny for America, who sail'd six Days before the Ellis, which is Arriv'd at Barbadoes, had an Insurrection coming over the Bar of Bonny, in which the Cooper and one or two Seamen were killed.

— October 8, 1776, Lloyd's List, London

The Vine, Jenkins, from Bristol, was cut away by the Negroes, on the Windward Coast of Africa.

— July 7, 1747, Lloyd's List, London

Those who live intimately with the dead experience the porosity of then and now...

– Saidiya Hartman, 2021

In the foreword to a government-commissioned report into racial disparities in the UK, slavery is dubbed 'the Caribbean experience'. While this unfortunate phrasing was picked up in the news, and its authors complained of missed contexts, at the heart of the story is a battle about how we portray empire and how we came to be here.

In the pursuit of counter-narratives, I sought out texts that allowed me to engage intimately with this history, with the dead. Because I could not approach the archive with cool detachment, I chose instead to deliberately seek connections with my own history, my contradictions and anger.

I had to find a doorway into these poems, working creatively with and against the records. I struggled with the Guipúzcoa agreement's officialese. It obscures the lives transformed – and wrecked – by it. I started by enquiring about the ship's name – the owner will have named it after the region of his birth – and to begin my quest for humanity there. I began listing questions which, of course, cannot now be answered, and decided to write a letter to the owner, Fermin de Tastet, which then became one of many emails.

The email sequence here is at first addressed to today's government report-writers with 'Jarrett ancestors' cheekily copied in. But what it contains is my attempt to subvert the language of banality – whether in work correspondence, contracts or academic texts – and embed/enmesh African deities, incantations, thought experiments and my own personal history.

In 'Faint and Fainter', the fading of the lettering as the language loosens could be suggestive of an expletive-laden continuation, or the slow and certain erasure of our history. My words literally sink into the whiteness of the page.

Overall, these poems are borne of mischief and trickery.

84. Faint and fainter (litany)

Chorus:
Litany for the unsung / Ballad of fleshmonger
Faint and fainter still my tongue / Let me not grow vulgar

1.
Scant the documents we grasp
The lives with/held within them
Is re/construction then our task?
Or reconciliation?

2.
A shanty or an elegy?
Disruption and subversion
Is how we'll broach this tragedy
Of inhuman perversion

Faint and fainter still my tongue / let me not grow vulgar

3.
Before the green, the black the gold
The greeting at Port Royal
A chain of *cargo* inspected
Uninsurrected spoil

4.
Boomeranged trajectory
Triangularly resigned
Here, ledgers of my ancestry
Conceivably were signed

Litany for the unsung / ballad of fleshmonger

5.
A layering of loss and wealth
Wielded in the shadows
Where Coffee House subscribers dwell
Hawking lives as cargo

6.
Slaughter then met sleight of hand
Hiding in forgetfulness
Underwritten apathy
A populace incredulous

Faint and fainter still my tongue / let me not grow vulgar

7.
Lombard Street's sun may have set
And empires have followed
Calls for redress yet unmet
Feigned innocence rings hollow

8.
Whataboutery runs deep
Seeping into the old stone
Heart of City's narrow streets
And foundations cast in bone

Litany for the unsung / ballad of fleshmangler
Faint and fainter still my tongue / let me not get angrier

9.
Mek we hush the duppy chile
Chewing on my marrow
Anger still unreconciled
Reckoning with sorrow

10.
Once the Nine Night have to end
Morning must take over
Bun de bloodclaat lot of
Babylonian Backra

Faint and fainter still my tongue / let me not get angrier

To: revisionism@uk.gov

Cc: Tony Sewell; Munira Mirza

Bcc: mum; 'The Jarretts'

Re: The Caribbean 'Experience'

Dear Reader,

To tell a tale requires a listener, and time, and a crossroads. To follow the red and black thread, the opening sky, the agitated *gallos* at dusk, to cross the muddy stream with a handful of keys and a flask at the whim of the teller demands trust. We have little to spare. Perhaps just enough. Perhaps not.

My plot summary (not attached) involves disappeared bodies, divine speculation and time-shifting. It ends where it begins, in the Old World. The protagonists unwittingly invoke ghost items while walking in the half-light, reading street names aloud. (This is, of course, entirely possible in the City: Fish Hill, Lime Street, Plantation Lane, Poultry, etc.) While humorous, it is ultimately a tragedy: unaware of their endeavours, they are doomed to stumble over what they've conjured/resurrected, leaping at shadows, misinterpreting the past in front of their eyes.

I have been advised, in my undertakings, to consider my own intimacy with the dead, and my relationship to other research material, far less innocuous. Sources include, but are not limited to, legalese designed to disguise human trafficking, and a whole bunch of dates, places, numbers, and miscellaneous data compiled as a list. Reading them aloud is nothing if not numbing, almost meditative: *The Betty, The Ogden, The Vine, The Louisa, The Juno…* ships and their travellers, bound and enslaved.

Need I say, clearly, I have skin in this? Trace my name to Manteca Bay, and its vast plantation. (A certain Colonel Nicholas Jarrett. A ship. An agreed sum. The trickery of flight.) This much can be inferred, the rest assumed. To address me is to unwittingly resurrect tall sugar cane fields, ships, coasts, ghosts, and, of course, insurrection. Lender agreements were signed off in these history-burdened streets that rippled out from Britain towards Caribbean shores. Presumably, one or more sealed the fate of some of my great-great-great-great-greats. But to tie this thread is contentious in this climate: likely to vex or perplex.

In my work, I have pursued the fugitive text, the speculative, the queer. At times, the non sequitur as a form of radical readjustment. Experience comes from *experiri* to try. I am trying not to reproduce violence, while addressing it from the margins. A hard bargain.

Our tale must then begin and end with its own masking. Ask an archivist and she will tell you much is hidden in banal documents. How the spectacle of blood, of executioners, of marrow and splinters flying, are muted in administrative language. How it is fudged and dulled by centuries of revision. How some truths may only keep the company of deep-sea deities.

Lately, I've been seized by a somnambulist compulsion (*Leadenhall, the Royal Exchange, Lombard Street, etc.*). Businesspeople come and go as the sun sets low behind the backs of glass buildings. My pocket jangles with my keys while I crisscross these streets, which offer neither redress

Nor easy conclusion.

Re: Guipúzcoa agreement

Hello Fermin,

I've been looped into this email so just jumping in.

I'm too tired for pleasantries. Where to even…?

This contract is… troubling? Puzzling?

I'm measuring my language, *claro*. Made a few napkin

calculations – or, tbh, used an online calculator tool to string

these numbers across our time continuums – to bring

you into the 21st and help with my mental labouring.

So, 'slaves valued at 45 pounds ea.' at a 1780 rate, taking in

today's inflation is roughly a 2017 value of – drumroll begin –

£3,454.25. These figures are… numbing? Astonishing?

But the rationale of trafficking is hardly worth imagining.

Fermin, honestly, do you feel you've struck a bargain?

Total ship value of more than a ¼ mil – it's staggering!

But do you feel the shiver of your future gathering

pace around the neck of these lands, laying

its hands on the soil over your grave, tightening

its grip for a reckoning?

To: buckrabuccanneer666@hotmail.com

Cc: fermindetastet1748@aol.com

Bcc: 'Keith's 2nd account'

Re: autoreply bounceback

Fermin,

I hope this finds you…

Well, I've been considering our predicament, the mismatch between your reality and mine and the context that permits a person of high standing to sign off captive humans as goods.

The precise complexion of goodness is a philosophical question; I refrain from specifically venturing those waters. Or, more plainly, despite this tentative address to you, I seek no redress from you, an unnecessary expending of both our energies.

Nonetheless, in my own lifetime, I have been privy to barroom conversations where beer-blurry men have argued till blue how we've all overblown the magnitude of endeavours like yours. These occurrences remind the writer how wretched wrongs get written off, its resounding echoes stretching from your time to mine, drowned by the din of ignorance.

For the purposes of this text, these concerns are neither here nor there while you remain *there* and I *here*. My queries are more exploratory, if you will.

I've been considering equivalents, to make sense of your situation: substituting the province of your birth, Gipuzkoa, with the borough of mine. Here I keep stumbling: purchasing an aircraft I dub *The Barking & Dagenham*; seeking Names to secure my expenditure, knowing this venture may be shot down mid-voyage; factoring in the kidnap of its passengers…

Further precision in this analogy is unfeasible; a disconnect between what's possible now and what was then: even should I wish, I couldn't legally land The Barking & Dagenham in the Caribbean, selling the people on to plantations… Here, and elsewhere, things fall apart (and I'm not sure this non-starter is the best use of my energy).

Nonetheless, this process of translation allows for a widening of conversation: from *data* and *document* to detailed *de*-detachment. With the imagination, possibilities are expanded. We scrutinise what it entails to be human. We sail on a path to deeper understanding. What the lists exclude we re-insert, reasserting the value of those rendered invisible. Beneath what you intended as a financial article, other complex lives become legible.

Once again, your value, for my purposes, is limited: beyond the briefest shadow I glimpse, cast from the mast of your ship over the vast breadth of ocean and time, you are irrelevant. I retain agency of my gaze, and you remain dead. The power once wielded in your favour is diminished. Empire is near-extinguished. We are learning to scour through its embers, reclaiming ancestors from ashes. We commemorate the captured, the capsizers, the survivors.

With or without us, time advances. The historian, and even the historian's child, will be long-gone history. The human body decays both on land and in the ocean. With it the human tongue, and any stain of language resting on its curl. Recollections dissipate within a lifespan. The recalling of pain ebbs like so many waves. The significance of objects fades as they face obsolescence, since we cannot all profess ourselves archaeologists. Even were we so inclined, the ribcage of the shipwreck at the bottom of the seabed has long-ago been devoured by worms. What has passed is rendered unfathomable. The fateful voyage once struck off in the Loss Book, less than a memory. The unpaid debt of all the names, uncrossed, as insignificant as a smudge on the ocean's surface. One man's attempt to double-cross the next, not footnote-worthy. Another's fabrication becomes a gospel. The rain falls and is unjust. It falls again, reformulates on farther coasts. A body of water, fragmented, replenishes the soil. Flags wave above muddy ground, are made impotent by the rain. On each side of the ocean, the earth clamours with our bloodshed. Lignum vitae proliferates on one side, oak thrives on another. Bones will be buried under both: mine and yours. What else must we do but excavate ourselves? With or without us, fragments surface above the waves. An article is returned, a reclaiming of a kind. Flotsam reconfigured, rehumanised. Our witnessing, another form of our reforming. Time advances, sea levels rise, and this ocean will soon signal the new season's arrival. The Atlantic grows restless in summer, as it has for many summers past. It is swollen with the poisoned history we have fed it. Or it is indifferent and shrugging. Or it is our grieving ancestors. Regardless, we seek out stories of our survival, our fleeting.

REMI GRAVES

The Betty, Duncomb, of London, was Overset and lost the 13th of March last, near Anamaboe on the Gold Coast. The Captain, Part of the Crew, and upwards of 200 Negroes were drowned.

– July 20, 1744, Lloyd's List, London

The Calvadas, ___, from Mosambique, is arrived at the Isles of France with the loss of about 50 Negroes by insurrection.

– February 19, 1793, Lloyd's List, London

Reading through the Lloyd's List, which catalogued what happened to trading ships, the ones that disappeared, the shipwrecked ones, those that were the sites of mutinies and uprisings, I was struck by the repetition of words like *'was lost'*, *'is lost'*, *'arrived at'*, *'held'*. The passivity of the language intrigued me, who lost the ships, how were they arrived? The differences in tenses used also struck a chord that ricocheted off the work of Christina Sharpe's *In The Wake* and Saidiya Hartman's 'The Time of Slavery', where both explore memory and time as non-linear in the context of slavery's ongoing legacy. I wanted my poems to contend with and speak to the inadequacy and indifference of the language of the catalogue. I was also deeply inspired by M. NourbeSe Philip's *Zong!*, and her auditory approach to language, and tried to experiment with using repetition and few words to capture the immensity and impossibility of the Middle Passage.

Alongside my immersion in the archive, which was not without its difficulties, I was reading Fred Moten's 'Fantasy in the Hold' chapter of *The Undercommons*. The fluidity and free association of his writing, as well as the concept of the hold as a space for imagination, refusal and freedom, inspired much of my thinking around these poems. At the same time, I started grappling with the question of the sea's victimhood, witness and complicity during the Middle Passage. It is amid this confluence of ideas that I tried to write these poems.

At the start of this project, I was interested in how abstraction could offer a kind of refuge from the violence and terror of the Middle Passage. How I might explore this impossible legacy at an angle of refusal. I'm not sure I managed to write consistently from a point of refusal, but in trying to I found conduits of thought and feeling that I'm still contending with.

calm seas

always moving
never ashore
never still
always dying
always alive
never alone
never not imagining
never not eyes to the overhead
never sky always overhead
painting blue beyond the hold
always dreaming
always always never never
always hearing the horizon tilt its axis
always knowing
the water beneath and above the buoying
never dry always parched
always imagining sated thirst
always thirsty
always damp never not
here always gone
always happened to never happened for
never not refusing
always refusing to never not refuse
always one foot on the bottom rung of the ladder, wrung mind, sea-swell, swollen hold, whole
in this ship's grubby grip hands slicked with tar, grit, shit, filth, salt, spit, vomit until elsewhere
becomes me — and what do we look like from up there, god's open air sitting room? a fleck of
something heinous on the good calm seas, tiny dark dots on un-cresting waves

gone

the sea has a thing on her lips
she's been longing   like us
for touch   company   some kind
of honesty for once

she's been breathless   run to seed
as if she too were whipped
wounded by her own complicity
slow moving pelagic thief   stretched

between rotten pier and wretched plot
there's no such thing as goodwater
in the tow of a saline taking
taste her crystal-guilt waterbody

those of us gone   to seed
crammed in the ship's hull
where nothing blossoms but the imaginary
burrow through damp wood to sky

how plant shoots root through soil
for breath
we have been holding each other
with our underwater hands

to learn of haptic frequencies
whilst the okra seed unflowered thing
dormant black bead of sweat past its time
makes soil of this drowned sea bed

gone

the sea has ▮▮▮▮▮ lips
longing   like us
for
honesty

she's been
whipped
wounded
slow   stretched

and

in the tow of a saline
crystal-guilt

those of us gone   to seed
blossom
through damp wood

root
for breath
hold
underwater hands

haptic frequencies
un
dormant black
soil

the sea

longing

for

wounded

b

y

gone

through

a vessel, unknown name

is / will be / was lost

hold

calm seas

hold

is arrived

hold

swollen

hold

a full slaved ship

hold

wind
hold
limb
hold
rains
held
cut off
sound beating the river's mouth and at by from to the

landed

LEVI NAIDU-MITCHELL

Letters from St. Kitts of the 23d of May advises, That the Negroes aboard the King David, Holland, from Old Calabar for St. Kitts, had Rose upon them near the Islands, and had kill'd the Captain and all the Crew, except four Sailors, who have carried the Ship into Guardaloupe.

– July 13, 1750, Lloyd's List, London

The Ann, Muir, from Africa to the West Indies, has been taken by the French, retaken by the Slaves, and carried into Martinico.

– July 7, 1797, Lloyd's List, London

Set in a hybrid world of the Caribbean shores and vastness of the Atlantic, this triptych's narrative can be viewed in any order. The centre canvas (shown on the right) takes place metaphorically in the Middle Passage, displaying the Mangrove tree. A concrete yet unruly and powerful plant, able to adapt in the worst of conditions, it acts here as a symbol of Black resistance. The Mangrove thrives in adversity, its roots both below and above water, creating an ecosystem and a sanctuary.

In the first canvas, an out of place Underwriter is seen hunched over their insurance risk book, determined and still writing even though they are far from their market room, whose tower of columns looms over them in the distance – the swinging bell begs the question: has it been rung once for ship lost, or twice for ship found*?

I have illustrated an overturned slave trading vessel in the third canvas (The Ship), with the remnants of a coffee house in the foreground. Coffee houses were known to be meeting points for merchants, ship-owners and seafaring persons and the remains of this coffee house are accompanied by steaming cups that have been seemingly abandoned. This signifies the unwavering will of the insurers, who continue to work even in the midst of destruction and shipwreck.

Viewed together, Canvases One and Three represent the holes in our knowledge, as we, the descendants of the enslaved, try to decolonise our heritage and piece together the puzzle of our history; when left without the full picture, we are plagued with endless questions. But in the context of the second canvas, the anchorage of the story is revealed. The Mangrove, flourishing furiously and vibrantly, represents our resilience and the crux of our story: the fact that raw and yet rooted, we remained and we resisted.

The Lutine Bell has hung at the centre of the Lloyd's Underwriting Room since 1858 and was traditionally struck once for a ship's loss and twice for a ship's return.

The Mangrove (Canvas Two)

© Levi Naidu-Mitchell

The Underwriter (Canvas One)

© Levi Naidu-Mitchell

The Ship (Canvas Three)

© Levi Naidu-Mitchell

JESS NASH

... The Society, Moneypenny, from Leverpool, is arriv'd at Annamaboe; and the Johnson, late Robinson, from Leverpool, at Logano, who had purchas'd 230 Slaves; but Capt. Robinson, the Doctor and his Mates, together with 17 of the Crew, were poisoned by the Negroes.

— June 29, 1764, Lloyd's List, London

The Nancy, capt. Williams, belonging to Liverpool as was mentioned in our list of the 20th Instant to have been cut off by the negroes, was cut about 8 o'clock in the morning, as she was lying at anchor at New Calabar, with 132 slaves on board, the slaves fell upon the crew and wounded several of them, the crew fired upon the slaves, killed 6 and wounded several more; but the natives that was on shore came off in canoes & surrounded the ship, and finding her weekly manned, having only five men on board but what were sick, they plundered the vessel and took the slaves out, some ivory etc. and then turned her adrift, the crew were taken up after by a boat belonging to capt. Labba, who was at anchor there.

— June 27, 1769, Lloyd's List, London

From the start of the project, I had a huge desire to unfurl a new narrative for the enslaved people, to give dignity back to them in some way. After the archive meeting at Lloyd's of London, I realised that I was really drawn to the Lloyd's List, in particular the accounts of vessels that didn't complete their journeys due to insurrection. There were so many enslaved people that fought back in strategic resistance, and that became my focus. From the List, I saw that many vessels trying to make it to New Calabar (Nigeria) and Annamaboe (Ghana, near Cape Coast) were unsuccessful in their trafficking due to insurrection. Whether that was due to the captain being poisoned on board the ship, or the ship never managing to dock before locals overtook it, it all started to give weight to the narrative of how intelligent and strategic locals were in their ability to completely overturn a well insured European vessel.

I'm very thankful for Gboyega who reminded me about the tone of the imagery and how others may read into the visuals I was putting forward. The three illustrations are based on my thought that the planning of a successful insurrection was probably done on shore, before they were captured. So, three ideas gave way to three illustrations:

'Community meeting' – where heads of the community could have come together to devise a plan and give out roles.

'The chefs' – the ones designated to learn how to slip poison into meals should they ever be captured and appointed as cook.

'Kroomen rescue mission' – as the abolition of the slave trade came nearer*, Kroomen worked to overturn vessels and bring enslaved people back to freedom.

*The UK abolished the slave trade in 1807, the USA in 1808; however other countries continued to trade throughout the 19th century.

Community meeting

© Jess Nash

The chefs, learning to poison

© Jess Nash

Kroomen - Rescue mission 1840

Kroomen rescue mission

© Jess Nash

COURTNEY CONRAD

Extracts of a Letter from Barbadoes, dated July 20, 1773. The Day before Yesterday came in the Betsey, Aird, with about 90 Slaves, from Sierraleon. Capt. Aird advises, that the Industry, of London, late Windsor, being on her Passage from Gambia to the West Indies, the Slaves killed all the white People except two, and carried her into Sierraleon, where they ran her on shore, and made their Escape; a few of them were taken, but Capt. Aird cannot tell what Number she left Gambia with. When the Insurrection happened one Gogart had the Command, Capt. Windsor having died on the Coast.

– September 17, 1773, Lloyd's List, London

Boston, April 27. On Friday inst. Capt. Stonehouse, of the sloop Betsey, arrived at Boston in 28 days from St. Thomas's. By her we learn that the ship Thomas, Capt. M'Neil, arrived at that island from the Isle De Loss, on the coast of Guinea, with a cargo of 200 slaves, between 40 and 50 perished on their passage by the disease and cruelties peculiar to this inhuman traffic. Capt. M'Neil's crew had been very sickly, the master, carpenter, cooper, and four other hands were buried in the course of the voyage.

– June 15, 1786, Daily Universal Register (London Times)

Throughout this project, I wanted to explore the conversations that were sparked before each sea voyage between slave traders and underwriters in coffee shops. Examining discussions about ship-board deaths and compensation, particularly the attitudes towards enslaved as humans seeking liberty, rather than just commodities. Additionally, I was committed to exploring the experiences from auction blocks to sea voyages specifically focusing on diet, disease and overboard disposal within the slave trade. Expounding from this lens I wanted to acknowledge the presence of women in the Middle Passage from capture to sale to transport: specifically, focusing on the intersectionality of their positionalities as mothers and wives, which compounded their efforts of escaping sexual violence and slavery through revolt attempts. Furthermore, I aimed to touch on the objectification of the enslaved whose lives were sometimes spared in order to retain wealth, but this still contained the dismantling of their humanity. Lastly, I wanted to speak to how those enslaved could humanise each other by bearing witness to each other's pain and as a result extending acts of kindness and sacrifice to enact love amid such unspeakable cruelty and White violence.

The following assisted these poems: '"Inherent vice": marine insurance, slave ship rebellion and the law' by Anita Rupprecht, *Dispossessed Lives: Enslaved Women, Violence, and the Archive* by Marisa J. Fuentes, 'Intimate History, Radical Narrative' by Saidiya Hartman, 'Intimate Inquiry: Love as "Data" in Qualitative Research' by Crystal T. Laura, 'Markup Bodies' by Jessica Marie Johnson, 'Accounting for "The Most Excruciating Torment": Gender, Slavery, and Trans-Atlantic Passages' by Jennifer L. Morgan and 'Not Your Average Coffee Shop: Lloyd's of London – A Twenty-First-Century Primer on the History, Structure, and Future of the Backbone of Marine Insurance' by Jeremy A. Herschaft.

Thank you to Spread the Word, Ink Sweat & Tears, Gboyega, Sasha, Pyar and Victoria for all the assistance.

Death Over Coffee

Before black pulses load vessels,
two men walk into a coffee shop
teaspoons stir the grit of dark beans
as curdling tongues spar. The underwriter
serves slave trader a platter of inherent vices:
malnutrition/disease/suicide/insurrection.
Slave trader knows ship carnages brew
long before rocking waves. Merchandise
readying for 'piracy'. Neither slave trader
nor underwriter willing to grind their shillings
over black fossilising villages underwater.

Two Hundred and Fifty Fine Healthy Negroes

church bell voices ring across the market square

only black gold sells here

        can I get   *can I get*

                 going once   *going twice*

                              sold   *sold*   *sold*   *sold*

ownership starts so young
even their grandsons buy nightmares
we board with other merchandise

beefbeefbodybodybodyporkpork
flourflourbodybodybodypeaspeas
ricericebodybodybodyyamyam

seventy-two days at sea, Captain says,
food and bodies better not spoil
the body eats the food it sells like

a diseased cargo
eroding at sea
the ship's horn

is our wailing choir
scurvy skin: a dark
sky with red spots twinkling;
rotten gums yearn for lime

juice-molasses-water
yellow fever mouths: chained
pipelines gushing sewage

after no. 92, the slave trader
listens to groaning pockets,
discarding the infested at sea.

Bait

Split / neither of us knows which tip of the triangle we will thread through / we are not witnesses to each other's boarding / on deck / I am unchained / with the other women / hoping my daughter is among us / and my husband below deck / opportunities for freedom are tangled but I stay prepared / prioritise feeding men whose arms are silvered in rage / and know how to fish for razors in stew / I am alive for Captain's pockets / the crewmen's blades and cocks / I have lost count of what night we are on / crewmen feast filthy and give no rest / sacrifice requires me to withstand the sharing / crewmen must holler over the breaking chains / their decapitations awaits / alongside my rest / that was how it was supposed to go / until Captain reeled in our attack / all men escape the ocean / but not the lashings / their bodies must sell half-healed / Captain brands me mastermind / hoists me up by my thumbs / for the sky to taste me too / the mouths under me hooked wide with sorrow / I reunite with my daughter / her wails ravishing my ears / I beg for Captain to take her into stillness with me / he points at her treasure womb before my release / I flounder waiting for a seabird God to snatch me up

Playdates for Sale

Mothers browse auction blocks for toys.
Our greased bodies on display with price tags
and trembling smiles. Each toy comes with
a whip that winds us up for longer-lasting playtimes.
A woman purchases me as a doll. I am hunched over
in a brown box with no manual. Before handing me over,
the salesman says, *No refunds. If broken, dispose of*
how you wish, perhaps, a play funeral could be fun.
Remember, 5% off your next doll.

I arrive at my new home, the woman tosses me
into her daughter's playroom. My unboxing
frightening, I peek my head out to see a small
ghost with gawking eyes in front of me. She does
not call me by the name my mama gave me but
by the one her mother shouts. Playtime begins swiftly.

We play 'Doctor'. Her father's shirt, a white coat.
His whip, a stethoscope around her neck.
I am the only patient. She asks where it hurts
and I want to say, "Where your mama burned me."
'Tea Time', she is a bakery owner serving
horse manure, mud and her father's piss.
I am a Rottweiler on all fours, tongue sticking out.
'Hide and Seek', I hide and her dogs hunt.
'Dress Up' ends the day. She dresses me as a runaway,
plucking my hair out like goose feathers, plants shrubs
in what is left of my afro and shreds my clothes.

After all this, I am her lullaby. My mama's stories
soothe her til my lips crack and she is snugged asleep.
I want to play a game where I am invisible and a child.

Stand Up in the Market Square with Neptune

Next on stage, a free Black man
getting his three hours of fame
after stealing an overseer's sheep
his mischief shepherding a fine
young lady back to his place.

"Y'all ever heard a jump rope knock? Shiiittt, I did.
Talkin bout *Open up, I'm gonna make you sway.*
His companion, a flat lip, limp dick duppy look-alike
who left holey. Later, his flock assembled
picked an executioner black like my damn daddy,
he might have been blacker but I ain't seen my daddy
since I left his balls and the white man took him."

A white mass before a negro
can make him feel like a saviour. Y'all cheer
while we make him uglier now, you hear.

"I'll cackle out my bones til I'm shapeless as your wives.
Speaking of wives, taste the meat they crave. Duppy
take my flesh for your sandwich.
I'll lift my head til I ain't got none
bet y'all wish you started with my tongue…

I've been Neptune."

More Blessed to Give

Between my legs, begging twists
seek renewal. Your hair strands
double dutch to our harmonised hymns
transplanting us to the Lord's feet.

Hunger lowers me into prayer. You come
with your last piece of communion.
Your flesh hangs like Christ's. I offer mine,
my wounds newly healed, I give you rest.

When my blistered fingers won't pick a pound more,
my sack of cotton brims with your extras. In the pit,
we take turns underneath the roof's slithering light
waiting to beam up to heaven.

Every good and perfect gift from each other.
Even if the Lord never frees us,
we don't set Him free.

MALAKAÏ SARGEANT

The Hope, Owen, from Bristol, is cut off at Benin on the Coast of Africa, and the Captain and Crew killed.

– April 30, 1762, Lloyd's List, London

That the Sloop Sisters, Jackson, had an Insurrection on board, and several were kill'd on both Sides. That a Ship belonging to London had carried off seven black Freemen from the Windward Coast, which has caused Disturbances in that Quarter.

– January 29, 1765, Lloyd's List, London

One of the things I think is true, which is a way of thinking about the afterlife of slavery in regard to how we inhabit historical time, is the sense of temporal entanglement, where the past, the present and the future, are not discrete and cut off from one another, but rather that we live the simultaneity of that entanglement. This is almost common sense for black folk.

How does one narrate that?

– Saidiya Hartman, 2018

With these poems, I wanted to explore, to borrow Hartman's phrase, 'temporal entanglement': how our histories leak into the present day, and how Black folk today exist in this twisted temporal haunting. Being exposed to the archives at Lloyd's – handling documents better preserved than the humanity in our history – served as a tangible reminder of the paradoxical existence of the African diaspora: being 'from' the same colonial metropole that played such a crucial role in our suppression. This process drew me to convene with the ghosts of my own and others' ancestors which, while affronting, reaffirmed to me that time, bodies, water and spirits are not linear. Each is a container for time, yet time still manages to pass through it. Black folk are like time, too. We cannot be confined, being too full of potential to be static. We are limitless and everything and nowhere all at once.

To tackle this realisation, I initially wanted to appropriate forms of European canonical poetry. This I did in one poem using the sestina – a form first documented in English in the sixteenth century – to highlight the rigidity and repetition laden within such writing against the repeated, cyclical horrors that Africans were made to endure during the trans-Atlantic slave trade (which, unsurprisingly, is difficult to find documented in the writing of Europeans during this period). When appropriating this form, I became more and more interested in purposely misconstruing other encounters I've had with archaic and pedantic English texts: contracts, crosswords and Bible verses are all forms I've used in these poems, satirising the sacredness of such texts, offering readers the chance to seek their own truths in the narrative. These poems, deeply inspired by untold stories tucked away in basements and behind paywalls, aim to shed a new light on how we have occupied time and space, transcendentally.

ON LOMBARD STREET

a brandished soul wails
between two walls on a terraced road,
searching for self in others
who have ended up here.
Meeting eyes with men
with shirts stained
underneath their blazers.
      What else are they hiding?
Trench coats   lined in a rouge wool,
underwriting abduction –
insuring legs
with limbs tethered to profit.
Tap-dancing along cobbled streets,
back-alley criminals
legalised by
shared interest: is
this the *Brave New World?*

                                    This, the brave New World!
Shared interest is
legalised by
back-alley criminals
tap-dancing along cobbled streets
      with limbs tethered to profit.
            Insuring legs;
underwriting abduction through
trench coats lined in a rouge wool.
What else are they hiding
underneath their blazers,
with shirts stained,
meeting eyes with men
who have ended up here,
searching for self in others
between two walls? On a terraced road,
a brandished soul wails.

A CROSSWORD FOR THE MIS-REMEMBERERS: BRITISH COMMERCE AND THE TRIANGULAR TRADE

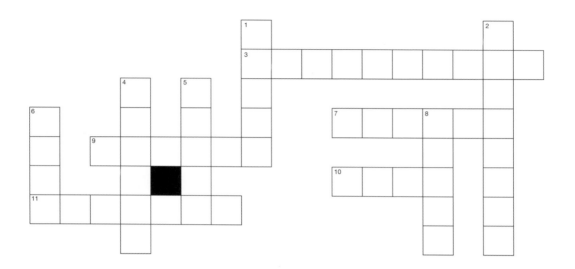

Across

3. britons badly conceal their jealousy at the french's ability to have executed this.

7. calloused foot bottoms are dyed this royal hue after a long day's labour.

9. clay blocks joined by a mortar of african blood.

10. part of a boat that stores crushed dreams, and bones.

11. invisible (read: intentional) genocide – avoidable if caught early and fatal if not.

Down

1. she embraced neoliberal free market economics, only to win no confidence among her peers.

2. roll the dice! flirt with new profits! collect £200 for passing 'go'!

4. location to trade deflating smiles, gossip, and other perishables.

5. arrivals and departures convene.

6. finite resource stolen from the motherland, notably at the coast.

8. a nation of tea and partition, settling across empire's re-imagined borders.

LAW CONCERNING SURVIVAL: CLAUSE 17.91

17.91.1 Somewhere in the Atlantic, right between
unnaming and reshaping,
is an African woman tied to a European chair.

17.91.2 The chair is naked, though bejewelled in weights, attached as anklets for
each splayed leg.

17.91.3 The woman is naked too,
her strained joints kissing
through gritted teeth.

17.91.4 Both items are insured, neither investment guaranteeing return.
Besides, the owners are much more concerned with the pursuit of other,
more refined brown things; to sweeten tea and liquor for parched thin lips.

17.91.5 Intertwined in the paradox of value against time,
even the woman's silhouette struggles, both shine and are shadow bound
to a mahogany coffin.

17.91.6 Sails of bloodied bandanas brandish the abandon of the horizon.

Here   is a woman,
naked–as she has been for an ashamedly long time–fastened to her own
autopsy.
A secret plunged into the tomb of the omega. Bloated organs tackle her
from the inside, exhausted from fighting   against the current.

17.91.7 They know that
if she's ever found,
no-one will be able to tell what form of paralysis killed her first.

STRIKE//THROUGH

Dear Almighty God,

if You are really / there, we pray that when / Your wind revisits, / distracted, necks snap / unexpectedly, as / if tapped on the back / by new destinies. / we pray for the heat / of guilt and pressure / to marry, walking the / devils down the aisle / to the tune of their / own failed abortion / for we prevailed / let us be merry, / at their expense, like / they do us, O Lord; / we lust to drink their / muffled screams in shells / recovered from home. / if You hear us now / give us just one thing: we ask for chaos ////
use Your hand to strike // through the black dove's cage // birth us in a new // darkness. //// let the air expand ///// let the sea gyrate ////// let the whole earth swell ///////// on this boat; the hold ////// like all of us here // is ready to burst.

Shall they rise? Indeed!

amen.

A SESTINA FROM THE INSURRECTORS

The Hope – 30.04.1762
Sisters – 29.01.1765
True Blue – 15.08.1769
Industry – 17.09.1773
Chance – 08.11.1776
Vigilant – 26.04.1791

We all knew when the time had come; we had no choice but to be vigilant.
The falsetto clanging of unhinged steel appendages could easily ruin our chance,
but the night was seasoned with ruin (and the Captain was inebriated). Hope,
the omniscient comrade for us captives in this industry,
was a siren curdling our blood cells, nursing our souls into re-existence. Sisters
blackened under a wayward sky, right now, exalted by the moonlight in a regal blue.

The Captain's eyes rocked with the boat, downing rum that connived to make blue
eyes sore and bulbous–akin to his sallow, pathetic skin. For these men, being vigilant
was a finite resource reserved for Spanish armadas or French revolutionaries; sisters
& co-conspirators on home turf but, when moored at sea & given half the chance,
would seek to battle over who had the monopoly in this industry.
Here, on this night, their marriage to indulgence kept crew distracted– & us hope-

full. For how many nights had we resisted heaven's whisper in the wait for hope's
arrival? She had come, swallowing a refrain of premature sobs, revealing the blue-
print to revolution in rounded palms. Plan hatched, we disintegrated into the dust,
making home across exposing ship floors. Tongues alight, premeditating the vigil
of the sea monsters, a war cry roared from the root of our bondage, chancing
with the devils as we collapsed their pedestals; pulverising & pounding & insist-

ing our way into the womb of a new tomorrow. It wasn't long before the stern
was convinced to join our side & began assisting our efforts with shopping
our souvenirs into the mouth of a watery tomb. Now, we were the law. No chancery
here to decide the sentence. Nor whip. No master with shrieking blue
veins and an odour as offensive to the senses as lant.
We'd rewritten this passage. And by all accounts, we turned our captors to dust.

How could it be thought that such creatures of punctured thought were ever ind-
ispensable? Somehow, even in death, the evil plastered in their faces subsists.
Laced arms swing in the breeze as dismembered heads spiral out to sea like lost lantana. Perennial monochrome blossoms dissolving into our tide of Black. Hopelessly
in decomposition. Salvaged only by accident. Souring the ocean's wail, lungs bluesy.
Yet, in all this un-anchorage, this amputation of errors, this delicious enchant-

ment of a ripe new day, there is more (& nothing) to be done. For what good is change
if only here? Our unborn would still be inscribed into sinews of fevered bones by an
industry
that rehearses lashings in cursive. 'X' still marking the spot. Illiteracy and stoicism
                    blooming.
Trapped in the middle of a prayer. Passing through at wits' end. Future in paralysis.
Yet, we cradled this unbeginning. We were always beyond reduction to mythopoe-
ic or fairytale. We've clawed through sinews of re-memory to reach you, to tell you,
                    gallantly,

>   we survived. Bound in a loveless placenta, we hatched our hope out of the blue,
>   out of sight and out of necessity. Vigilant, searching for cracked irises, we took the
>   industrious out one by one. Together, as sisters, we took the chance.

wi meh be likkle, but wi tallawah.

THE SERMON ON THE MOUNT

poor   spirit,   kingdom of

those who mourn,   comfort

the meek,   they will

hunger and thirst

.

for   mercy.

they will see

peace,   for they

are persecuted.

you   insult

evil   because of me. rejoice!   because   in

heaven,   the   persecuted   prophets who were before you

can   be made

again. It is   good   to be   out, a

light of the world   not   hidden.

NOTES & GLOSSARY

Keith Jarrett Introduction   *Page 12*

a government-commissioned report: 'The Commission on Race and Ethnic Disparities' was set up in the summer of 2020 by Munira Mirza, then head of the Number 10 policy unit under Prime Minister Boris Johnson. The Commission's chair was Dr. Tony Sewell. Its report was published in March 2021 to widespread criticism.

'84. Faint and fainter (litany)'   *Pages 13-14*

duppy (West Indian) – a malevolent spirit or ghost

Nine Night – an African-derived Caribbean funerary tradition extending for nine nights following a person's death, which includes music, food and rituals. On the final night, the deceased's spirit must be expelled from the home by rearranging their mattress and other furniture.

bloodclaat (Jamaican) – a vulgar, emphatic expression, usually employed idiomatically to express anger or frustration. Literally: 'blood cloth'/sanitary towel.

backra or buckra – slaver or overseer. It is used in different ways in Caribbean and Southern US English/es, sometimes referring to anyone in power, to systemic oppression, or a White man more generally, depending on context.

'To: revisionism@uk.gov'   *Page 15*

Cc: Tony Sewell; Munira Mirza: see note on Commission above.

gallos (Spanish) – cock/rooster

Jess Nash Introduction   *Page 38*

Kroomen – a group of people originally hailing from Liberia that came to settle in Freetown, Sierra Leone. They were Kru speaking, expert navigators and boatmen. When the West African squadron came into its heyday, after the 1807 Slave Trade Act abolition of the industry, Kroo men became 'Kroomen'. A fierce opposition to the trade was at the core of their identity.

'A CROSSWORD FOR THE MIS-REMEMBERERS: BRITISH COMMERCE AND THE TRIANGULAR TRADE'

Page 56

References and paraphrases information from Chapter 3 of Eric Williams' 1944 book *Capitalism and Slavery*.

Answers:

Across	Down
3. REVOLUTION	1. TRUSS
7. INDIGO	2. MONOPOLY
9. BRICKS	4. MARKET
10. HOLD	5. DOCKS
11. DISEASE	6. GOLD
	8. INDIA

'THE LAW CONCERNING SURVIVAL: CLAUSE 17.91'

Page 57

Inspired by and written in response to Sowande' Mustakeem's essay: '"She must go overboard & shall go overboard": Diseased bodies and the spectacle of murder at sea'. *Atlantic Studies*, Vol. 8, No. 3, September 2011, 301-316. The title of the poem is after Kei Miller's 'The Law Concerning Mermaids' (2010).

'A SESTINA FROM THE INSURRECTORS'

Page 59

Conceived after trawling through the Lloyd's List and counting the number of insurrections recorded in that period, of which there were 39 between 1744-1820. malakaï chose six of the names of the ships where insurrections occurred and formed the thirty-nine-line poem as a result.

lant – aged urine, historically used for cleaning and laundry because of its ammonium content

lantana – a plant of the verbena family native to tropical parts of the Americas and Africa. (Gorgeous flowers but with leaves that are poisonous to most animals. Can be invasive.)

wi meh be likkle, but wi tallawah (Jamaican patois) – we may be small, but we're strong-willed

BIOS

Gboyega Odubanjo (editor) was born and raised in east London. He is an editor of *bath magg* and the author of two poetry pamphlets, *While I Yet Live* (Bad Betty Press, 2019) and *Aunty Uncle Poems* (Smith | Doorstop, 2021).

Dr. Keith Jarrett's work explores Caribbean British identity, religion and sexuality. A multiple poetry slam champion, he was selected for the International Literary Showcase as one of 10 outstanding LGBT writers in the UK. His poem, 'From the Log Book', was projected onto St. Paul's Cathedral and broadcast as a commemorative installation. His play, *Safest Spot in Town*, was performed at the Old Vic and aired on BBC Four. *Selah*, his poetry collection, was published in 2017. Keith teaches at NYU in London and is completing his debut novel.

Remi Graves is a London based poet and drummer. A former Barbican Young Poet, Remi's work has been commissioned by St Paul's Cathedral, Barbican and BBC Radio 4. Remi has taught at The Poetry School and performed at Cheltenham Literature Festival, Tate Modern and more. Remi's debut pamphlet *with your chest* was published by Fourteen Poems in 2022.

Levi Naidu-Mitchell is an interdisciplinary artist, currently based in London. Her practice centres around the Carnivalesque, its dynamism as an artistic medium and the plethora of ways it can be translated as a tool for positive, vibrant elevation. Workshop facilitation, collaboration, community, site specific and socially engaged projects are all fundamental to her creations and she deems it essential to work intergenerationally, always considering the living archive, ancestry and the legacies that we produce through our art.

Courtney Conrad is a Jamaican poet. She is an Eric Gregory Award winner, Bridport Prize Young Writers Award recipient and has been shortlisted for *The White Review* Poet's Prize, Manchester Poetry Prize and Oxford Brookes International Poetry Prize. Her poems have appeared in *Magma*, *The White Review* and *bath magg*, and her work has been widely anthologised. She is an alumna of The London Library Emerging Writers Programme, Malika's Poetry Kitchen, Barbican Young Poets, Obsidian Foundation and Roundhouse Poetry Collective.

Jess Nash is an illustrator whose work is based on her love of culture and social commentary. Working across different areas of illustration and animation, her goal is to create moments of relatability, connection and joy. She's had the pleasure of collaborating on projects with VANS X MoMA, Penguin Random House and the Design Museum.

malakaï sargeant is a writer, theatre director, dramaturg and cultural producer from pre-gentrified Hackney, London. Led by curiosity and care, malakaï creates and interrogates through an unapologetically Afroqueer lens. They are a senior producer at Poet in the City and Co-Creative Director of experimental literary arts organisation BORN::FREE.

CORE PARTNERS

Black Beyond Data brings Digital Black Studies, computational humanities, and community engagement together. The shared goal? Humanising, repurposing, and activating data and conversations around data for the Black freedom struggle and Black study more broadly. Black Beyond Data work occurs alongside and across three interlocking pillars, ones particularly relevant in this current moment, but timeless in their impact: health data, slavery and data, and Black community data. Black Beyond Data is supported by the Mellon Foundation.

blackbeyonddata.org

Underwriting Souls, developed by Alexandre White and Pyar Seth of Black Beyond Data and based at Johns Hopkins University, is a set of digital exhibits and materials examining the role of insurance in the trans-Atlantic Trade through objects within the Lloyd's Archive. In March of 2022, Lloyd's of London and Johns Hopkins University entered into a research collaboration agreement that protected academic freedom and integrity as central to this project. As part of this agreement, Lloyd's of London has not and will not provide funding for the project. Lloyd's bears no editorial right over the final language, form or presentation of the digital products produced. Victoria Lane is Lloyd's Archivist and has worked closely with Alexandre and Pyar; work on any final materials will be produced in collaboration between Lloyd's, Victoria Lane, Alexandre White and Black Beyond Data.

underwritingsouls.org

Spread the Word is London's literature development agency, a charity and a National Portfolio client of Arts Council England. Founded by Bernardine Evaristo and Ruth Borthwick, we develop the careers and creative talents of London's underrepresented writers. We have a national and international reputation for initiating change-making research and developing programmes that have equity and access at their heart. Through partnerships with people and organisations driven by a shared vision to diversify the stories that we read and hear, we help enrich the UK's literature ecology.

spreadtheword.org.uk/uprising-resistance

Ink Sweat & Tears is an online poetry and prose web zine run by Kate Birch and edited by the poet Helen Ivory with a small print publishing arm whose pamphlets have been shortlisted for major poetry awards. Chloe Elliott and Prerana Kumar, who both lent their expertise to the project, have been part of the Ink Sweat & Tears editing internship programme.

inksweatandtears.co.uk